LIGHT IN, LIGHT OUT, LIGHT STAYS

Chamkaur Gill

This collection of poems

is dedicated to Bee Chen,

the rhapsody who is my wife

and Mindy, the symphony

who is our daughter.

Here's to words

that skim across the surface

of the reader's consciousness

and perceptions,

and to those that dip into

the sub-surface of mine.

CONTENTS

I

RING, FALTER, FADE

Recollections

———

Quiet ruminations on the ledger of times gone
Lift ancient truths out of deserted rubble,
Easing recollections of upended yearnings.
Kindred fretfulness and goodwill
Echo bitterness and wry smiles.

Quiet chuckles soften battle-scars.
Hazy mists delicately blanket dismay and angst,
Whispering calm over once-intense emotions.
Eye-balling evolves into amiable gazes.

Triumphant and pyrrhic victories,
Fingers entwined, no more, no less.

Masks and nakedness simply dim images,
Blended into singularity.
Adversity and triumph sit leaning against each other.
Mixed feelings in cupped hands.
All we had, all we missed,
Merely old races run.

Like related neurons, distant and close memories
Thread their textures into each other.
A genial parity achieved,
The then embraces the now in kinship.

Light

———

Our times come, they go.
Other times begin.
Sounds of glory ring, falter, fade,
Their echoes falling, and then rising again,
Blossoming into new sounds.

Light in, light out,
Light stays.
A shimmering glow flickering dull and bright,
Palpitating ceaselessly.

It is the way of the world
That the here and now is feted,
While the seed withers and perishes,
Replaced by its kin.

What beauty can fresh blooms radiate,
If it is not relinquished by parting petals?
To begin, it ends.
To end, it begins.

A relaxed stoop

—

The fluidity of the waking hours;
Time without compartments;
Restrictions lifted and schedules shelved;
All become the new normal.

Shoulders ease into a relaxed stoop
With gravity bequeathed to youth.
The furrowed brow softens into quietude.
The amassed multitude of passions
Consigned to limbo,
Fingers, once feverish, now interlock sitting back.
With aspirations breasted,
A slow jog ensues, culminating in a slow stroll.
It, too, will have its end.

But lingering uncertainty questions
The creak of the shutting door.
A brief glance back.
It would be a curious return.

Shell

———

Thinning thread on a fading spool,
Unheralded in the mass,
Inconspicuous.

Just one of a few leaves left on the tree,
Alone, devoid of its milieu,
Drying in the sun.

Overtaken, left behind in the outside lane,
Visage gradually fading in the rear-view mirror.
The inconsequential, fuzzy periphery of salad days
Shuffles backwards towards the finish line.

Elasticity has shrivelled.
Throbbing rigidness, once a staple of suppleness,
Is consigned to the past,
Replaced by the flaccidity of the arthritic shell.
Soft and stiff, stiff and soft.

Fires of passion reduced to dying embers.

Sagging flesh on leathery tendons.

Slumped muscles on brittle bones.

Wooden fingers on trembling hands.

The body's withering, end-game rhythm,

Awaiting its ebbing into the universe.

The final page

——

My gratitude, life, for your companionship 24/7.
You have not nudged me
In a direction of your choosing,
Nor have you heralded what lies ahead
(Or do you also not know?),
Preferring, instead, to let moments turn like pages.

The smiles, guffaws, tears, sobs
Are learning pathways etched on my face,
Created in your presence as you walk with me.
Losing hair, gaining face, gathering barnacles.
Still some discovering to do
As our trek approaches its completion.

When we are almost done with my book,
And it is time to go our separate ways,
I hope for a firm handshake from you
Before I gently loosen my grip and depart.
The final page will reveal whether I'll miss you.

Pangs

———

Ah, De Quincey, these keen, lancinating pangs,
Marked by indifferent neglect in our youth,
Seem increasingly, in old age, more disquieting.
Their arrowy stabs signalling inescapable decline,
Throbbing radiations swell relentlessly,
Unconfined burning twinges that drain blood.

Glancing jabs that crucify the body
Forfeit the premium of effortless days.
Thrusting spears of radiating torture lie in ambush,
Striking the unaware remorselessly
With violent spasms of anguish.
Ferocious agony, causing shuddering halts,
Torments in splitting moments.

Stop

———

Lifting, lowering, pushing, pulling.
Seven.
Feeling prodding, stroking, pointing.
Six.
Walking, running, gliding, stomping.
Five.
Stretching, bending, enduring, kneeling.
Four.
Crooked, supported, served, defended.
Three.
Borne, rotated, flexed, extended.
Two.
Resolve crippled.
One.
Slow, slow, stop.
Done.

Journey

Millions of completions,

Each tethered to its own stopwatch,

Cannot halt time.

Moments multiply within their frame,

As they tick farther away from the start.

Hours approaching completion

Watch the timekeeper sign off on the billboard.

Each final chime signals fulfilment

As the timepiece calls it a day.

Event by event, the road rolls along,

Unhindered.

Even when the pendulum stops.

The psyche lags

The distances created by the still-to-grow
Stretch back to the beginning.
Memories rumble with echoes of agitation,
Slowly planting tremors remorse cannot fight.
They return, the weaknesses,
As quickly as they depart.

The psyche lags in the body's marathon.

Ageing is not always rewarded with mellowness
And wisdom often eludes antiquated reasoning,
Demanding validation in graven armchairs,
Blinded Cyclopes flinging tempestuous thunderbolts.
Baying at the moon, scarred craters dig deeper,
Craggy faces gouged and hardened by intractable will.

Wither

———

Parched weed in the pitiless grip of the callous pot,
You have no ally in the sky.
The grey clouds flaunt their wealth as they drift by
And the sun blazes its disdain.

You are mocked by the languid drips of the tap,
Slowly moistening the silver concrete.
The oblivious bottle sitting static next to you
Is deaf to your pleas.

What use is resolve in the face of capitulation?
Accept your shrivelling.
No more supple limbs, pliant in dainty clothes.
Petrified in brown.

Your green has sunk into your little dry plot,
Your grave.

Joints

——

Reaching, extending, stretching, rotating.
Pushing, pulling, lifting, lowering.
Spinning, turning, twisting, gyrating...
...keep adding.

Nimble, flexible, loose, relaxed,
Agile, lithe, brisk, spry,
Lissome, supple, limber, pliant...
...don't stop.

And then... it starts fading,
Irrevocably.

Straining, shrinking, stagnating, stiff.
Hesitating, deterred, mortified, brittle.
Arthritic, rheumatic, inelastic, thick...
...too much.

Ossified, petrified, solidified, rigid
Wooden, impliable, immalleable, hardened,
Frozen, benumbed, contracted, unsupple...
...no more.

And so ... the sentence ends,
Inevitably.

Faded photo

___

The single moment in the faded photo
Conceals the before and after.
The life, the passions, the aspirations -
Traced in private stillness, forever hidden.

What led to the pose, the mien?
Once accomplished, what transpired?
Millions of other moments lie buried,
Their tales extinguished by the ages.

Silent echoes of concluded prospects
Create muffled imaginings in rigid pose.
The inner eye momentarily visualizes life
In the motionlessness of black and white.

Emptiness

No more the soft breast
Where the cheek rested.
Now just the cane's crook,
Cold, hard, cold-hearted.
Ageing eyes gaze blankly
At unresponsive emptiness.

Struggling memories recall
The affection of tenderness.
Endearment, once warming,
Shivers in its stony gloom.

All fade into reminiscence.

Desolate spaces ignore tears,
Cold silence sits wordlessly,
Apathetic, indifferent, distant.
The warmth of love is no more,
Its forlorn embers numbed,
Extinguished by abandonment.

Paper boats

The paper boats of our lives' stages
Float away singly on gentle streams.
They carry with them our vicissitudes,
Our lives' bounties and retributions.
No keels, no rudders, no tillers impede
Their fragile hulls as they drift beyond.

For a while, we walk alongside,
Keeping an eye on what they meant.
In due course, they move out of sight,
Disowning ever-waning shadows.
Yet, their whispers remain in our minds,
Distant echoes of receiving and losing.

Wheel

Effortless passage, once presupposed,
Now stumbles with lead-footed labour
And roaming has lost its nimbleness.
Excitement falters as fatigue approaches,
Wielding an ominous spanner
While stagnation edges out ardour.
Sleek manoeuvres have lost their zest.
Fluid rhythm is fading away.
The wheel nears its conclusion.
How many more spokes to turn?
When will the hub grate to a halt?
Shiny, then greased, now rust.

II

FARTHER DIMENSIONS

Decided?

———

Are miracles decreed?

Does destiny have a formula,
Or fate a blueprint?
Does possibility have a compass,
Or probability a circumference?

Can luck be calculated,
Or coincidence stipulated?
Where is the math in karma,
Or the science in kismet?

Is there a pattern to providence,
Or a design behind fortune?
How do we quantify preordination,
Or determine predestination?

Is there a method to chance,
Or a system in prediction?
Can one's lot be enumerated?

Is coincidence intended?

Is divine will computed?

The searcher

———

The true searcher sips from many fountains,
Declining invitations to conform.
What? Why? cry the decriers,
Frantic in their ensconced confines,
Ritualising in parenthesis,
Consumed by the exclusive.

Those holier would have you plant your feet,
Barricading against consciousness.
Narrowed divinity confined under a glass bowl,
Like sand in an hour-glass.
Grace is condemned by the gallows' hood.
Ignorant of the inclusive.

Eyes on the horizon perceive more
Than downcast eyes.
Unshackled steps traverse inside and out.
Unfettered strides cross boundaries.
Enabling flight spreads wings.

Books upon books, the word multiplied.
A multitude of voices singing in unison,
Proclaiming many truths,
Soaring, not stifled.
Breathing, not suffocated.

New times

The departed moment is done
But the minutes in the vastness ahead
Shall meet it again
When they retrace their steps
And guide its revival with each visit.

Its soul, merged with others to form a giant light,
Will reappear to shape new times.
And soar to new heights,
Taking zeitgeist into farther dimensions.

Consciousness will arise from the corporeal
And reveal the limitlessness in the moment,
Providing insight upon further insight.
A multitude of instantaneous epiphanies
Will encompass the fleeting and the everlasting.

Wretched mea culpas

———

I've sinned, said the mortal
Who knew she was sinning.
Candle-wax under a tired flame,
Questioning its misfortune,
Morphs into a distorted realisation,
While fire-ants climb all over it.

The scab that conceals the wound
Is a thin veneer for transgression.
Guilt wears a barefaced mask
That transparent hands cannot veil.
No flight behind confining curtains
That cling to the exposed guise.

Wretched mea culpas ring hollow,
Whirlpools swirling into a dark abyss.
No salvation in self-chastisement.
Clemency glares balefully at her,
Grace wrung in its pitiless hands,
And summons self-crucifixion.

God appears fleetingly, faceless, silent.

S(he) does not touch her.

Teacher

———

Bloodied on the road, the light grows dimmer
And then lifts itself through an inner glimmer
That hums with a quiet resonance
And rises to a harmonious crescendo
Which cascades over rocky mountains
And lifeless deserts
And dense forests,
Without being blighted by the ego.

Words that dance in harmony with the stars,
Lift many, yet leave many with scars,
Travelling vast distances from the source
That was the first to feel their heartbeat,
On willing feet that never run their course,
Through deserts
And dense forests,
Conciliatory in the realm of conceit.

What tingling brought about the reverberations
That lifted the curtain?

Would it have been wiser to stay in lethargy
Than to be drawn towards the spotlight?
The starlight of fire-flies escapes reproach,
Unlike the searing flame of enlightenment.
What tragedy, what triumph in scorched wings
That live within lives and grow without growth!

Fertile vessels abound with celebrations,
While the barren ones remain uncertain.
Beaming genially with boundless synergy,
Benevolence reaches out to spite.
Despite walls that glare balefully at approach,
The enduring message defies imprisonment.
Living and dying, the instrument sings
Embraced and shunned as it goes forth.

Nanak

———

The thread of mercy, contentment,
Self-restraint and truth
Unravelled the customs of rigid times,
And, denying the eastern sun
The blessings of the river,
Dampened the fire of rituals.
Established dogma paled at the feet of Naam.
New knowledge spun
In the realm of unknown constellations,
Gifted by an indescribable bestower,
Whose name is chanted
By multitudes of tongues, millions of times,
Keeping the five thieves at bay.
The mind's eye witnessed the true essence
Of the undefinable,
The timeless, shapeless, nameless,
Self-generated dynamism,
Unseen originator of the visible and the invisible
Who walk the earth,
Ageless, classless, united in the presence

Of an eternal, divine light,

That presides over beginnings and endings.

One.

It was the certainty

That the illuminated mind discerned.

Reality.

It was the path

That defined the essence of enlightenment.

Thieves

———

There is no want in the serpent's strike
Or the animal's kill.
Only exigency.
So, what of the hedonism that rages within us?

Kaam rages with a passion that throbs with lust,
Snatching sense from rational thought.
Calm the prowling monster with serenity.

Krodh rears its snarling head in fury,
Shredding unsuspecting serenity to bits.
Convert your passion into harmony.

Lobh palpitates with uncontrolled greed
Stealthily gaining ground against contentment.
Guard against avarice and less will become more.

Moh, the cache gatherer, is anchored to possessions,
Generous only unto itself.
Nurture your soul and let love attach itself to you.

Ahankar wears entitlement like a crown,
Unwary of the encroaching ego's silent footsteps.
Look beyond yourself and find generosity within.

Want retreats when Naam is heard, says the Guru.

Pathways abound

The dreary demands of spiritual chains
Clank ever louder,
Tyrannizing devotion.

The sheen of untethered prayer radiates, too.

Unvarying animation drums nagging patterns
Ceaselessly,
Dictating supplication.

Worship-halls waiting within hum soothingly.

Uncontrollable nervous tics
Replay meaningless motions,
Eyes closed.

The destination calms through its many doors.

The deadening tourniquet
Squeezes the free-flowing spirit,
Denying growth.

Let the captain in each unfurl the sails.

Yoked oxen trained to tread the same path
Trudge mutely,
Without question.

Pathways abound, straight or meandering.

Trapped in its wheel,
The hedgehog scampers nowhere,
Silently fragile.

Let feet find heightened grounds, un-enslaved.

Frozen water cannot flow.
Confined breezes cannot blow.
Invisible embers cannot glow.
Potted plants cannot grow.

Possessing God

——

Accept your impurities.
Doesn't God belong to all
In all ways,
Always?
Why should God be circumscribed property,
To be stored by hardened zealots?

Enhance your goodness.
Spread inherent godliness.
Why compartmentalize God?
Is faith defined by possessing God?
Isn't God undiscriminating, unrestricted?

Be good.
Do good.
Know God.
Is God not everything and everybody,
Female and male?

Be an -ism.

Why isolate God?

Can't God be reached in every way,

By everyone,

Everywhere?

Gift

The light of the Eternal One shone again
When you were gifted to the world.
As with many of the Creator's chosen,
The Illumination was channeled through you.

Clarity showered its brightness everywhere,
Radiating into the fog of shadows.
Your shimmering Message opened eyes
And lifted the shroud that choked Truth.

You incurred the wrath of the unbending
With fortitude in the face of rejection,
And calmness in questioning empty customs.

You sought no glory in elevating the Name,
Preferring to praise It as humanity's salve.
Agitated fences fell in your noble presence,
Overcome by your words of profound wisdom,
Delivered to you from an Infinite Domain.

Casting aspersions

———

What would you make of today
If you were to see what's changed?
The thread of tradition has morphed
Into symbols of exclusivity.

Tolerance has surrendered to disdain
And contempt ridicules forbearance.
The simple path to the True Being
Is yet again tangled in sinuous knots.

The One is pulled in every direction,
Each claimant declaring pre-eminence
And erecting roadblocks on the portal,
Casting aspersions on the antagonist.

Meaningless rituals handcuffed to time
That you wisely proclaimed against
Have reshaped their glorified lives
In processions and venerations.

Warring voices clamour for ownership,
While bodily ablutions relegate the soul.
Faith in virtuous toil, serving and sharing
Lies trodden underfoot, Illusion's victim.

The hands of the mellow believers
Are helpless against pitiless boulders.
How many more saintly re-emergences
Before the powerful venerate the ant?

Pious

———

Mortals paying homage to hollow rites
Pervert the truth in divine bestowal.
The virtuous design contained within
Sits alone, ignored, deserted, unwanted.

Unrighteousness continues unabated,
Transgressions flourish unconstrained.
Devotional aspirations are desecrated,
Befouled blindly, victimised by denial.

Self-consecrated godship wields a whip
That sacred ambition never coveted.

The simple truth

Bright lights, day and night,
Swirling clouds,
Flowing beards,
Haloed visages,
Faceless messages,
Glowing softness,
Paramount immortals,
Outward sanctitude,
Indiscernible symbols,
Strident bells,
Clarion calls,
Virtuous counsellors,
Revered manuals,
Doctrinal exhortations –
In the midst of these reverberations,
Listen to the silent whisper of the simple truth.

III

THE BLINKERED MIND

The burning fox

————

Where the burning fox
Reshapes itself as poisonous fangs,
The minions of foretold evil gain strength
Through malignant messages.

The embodiment of malevolence
Feared by the believers
Is not a 1
But the sum-total of the instruments of transmission,
Disseminating to decimate.
Feeble minds fall prey
To the sixth, the fifteenth and the twenty-fourth,
Which, in their triplet incarnation, arm the devious
With insidious declarations and biased revelations,
Making untruths truths and truths, untruths.

Rabble-rousing is the untethered norm.
Self-serving intentions target open-endedness,
Seeking to impose dominance and supremacy.

Abusive thoughts and villainous acts are moulded

By malicious narrations that dive and soar insidiously,

In the guise of myopic sentiments,

Tainting the noble emblem.

Misstep

———

Nobody remembers your apology, fighter,
Only your arrogance and its price.
Your crowing has ended in ruffled feathers.

Heaven's a long way away from the floor
And your desolation goes unheeded.
Your contrite whimper remains unheard
As the world derides your silenced roar.

The pinnacle is a needle-head
And no zenith exists without a nadir.
The wilting of your sneering chest
Is cause célèbre,
While Glee cackles at your remorse.

Detachment

———

Neighbourliness,
Partitioned by incompatible privacies,
Mutedly resides in blurred, inoffensive vagueness,
Satisfied by truncated salutations extended fleetingly.
One world suffices.

Perfunctory glances for the briefest of seconds
Underlie mutually beneficial acceptance
Of detachment.
We slink into ourselves.

Cagey comings and goings prolong hibernation
And ensure needless entanglements are kept at bay.
Keep things uncluttered.

Wary eyes cast downwards dart briefly,
Hoping for the absence of presence.
Being, not seeing.

Nervous dispositions,
Becalmed by encompassing limits,
Elude unsettling anxiety
Lurking outside sheltered boundaries.
No audience effect.

Hurriedly entering the safe space,
Breathing eases behind the door.
Until tomorrow.

Rapacious fingers

Deprivation seeks concealed panacea
Barricaded by the selfish machinations
Of dominion.
Rapacious fingers, contorted to seize,
Throttle succour.
Lascivious hands, bloated with avarice,
Veins throbbing with the blood of greed,
Open only to those who have
And those who have to accede,
Squeeze every iota of essence,
Constricting deliverance.

Wily minds

———

Narrowed eyes that guide the tongue
Finger words that hear the scent.

Single mind perched on indoor plant,
Screened from outdoor trespass,
Picks moments of promise to skim
Over substance overlaid with a thin veneer
Of web that snags like quicksand
And enmeshes fleecy sheep
In bottomless quagmires.

Enticement deceptively seduces the unwary
Into the wily minds of containment.

The craning neck lords over the grains
That lie de-husked in the mortar
While the pantomime wand waves
At empty skies
And distracts trusting togetherness
From streams flowing
Into secret, select holds.

Cage

———

In suffocating the winged thoughts of spontaneity,
You choke the air out of progress.

When wings are grasped by unrelenting hands
And kept from unfurling for free flight,
Nature's grace is denied its bountiful growth.

You have not won your throne by killing kings.

The chameleon smiles at bowed heads.

How does power devise irons that bind
And yet not see how they leash inspiration?

Imprisoned verses turn to bone.

What lack of thought governs obstinacy
That it cannot see the cruelty of the cage?

Smothered beauty cries out for room.

Why does the blinkered mind enshrine possession,
Diminishing the pulse
Of free-flowing natural instinct?

Enclosures fossilise the spirit.

When will stunted judgement be rid of its infancy
And unclog each pore of the moss that gags wisdom?

Bled-out release floats stagnantly.

Devoid of lustre

_____

Infernal sounds rising in screeching crescendo

An incessant tsunami of noise

No diamonds dropping off the tongue

Grating cacophony of incomprehensible clamour

Invading space with ear-splitting screeches

Scurrying voices crashing into each other

A hateful din comprehensible only to them

Decibels assailing the soul

Disarranging patterns

Motorbike in a blender

Until

I caught a glimpse of my soul

And saw it devoid of the lustre in theirs.

The strutting ego

———

The hands that embody the small mind
Incorporate the limitations of one so blind
That portents are belligerently disregarded
In arrogant vanity, all sagacity distorted.
The strutting ego, overbearing, high-handed,
Invades logic, infantile wit flaunted,
Then swaggers, pompous, cradle-nourished,
Into puffy conceit, smug, undistinguished.

The disequilibrium in an unpredictable head
Intrudes upon dignity, and reasoning has bled.
Those counselling sanity are rudely discarded,
Inconsistent grasp obtrusive and bloated.

The grating voice sneers turgidly, orotund,
Inflated hubris a prelude to the moribund.
Thus does tyranny, preeminence-consumed,
Invoke foreboding visions of ethos doomed.

Supremacy

Glib narratives, repeated instantaneously,
Pollute unsuspecting minds en masse.
Fraudulent intent, screened from scrutiny,
Darts on the wings of indoctrination,
Habituating thinking with fake idolatry.

Serpentine supremacy lords over devotees.

Self-aggrandisement postures in false glory,
Appalling common decency with abandon.
Smirking smugness chafes and irritates.

No gentility dwells in the age of Kaliyug.
It conceals a secret design of evil cunning,
Channeled through its blustering offspring
Whose unhinged mind fathoms falsehoods,
Sanctimoniously, to be beyond reproach.

Foolhardy disregard

———

The dictates of self-importance create barriers
Which rise ever higher against benign wisdom,
Confronting sound counsel with blind dismissal,
Rebuffing the certainty of calamitous implosion.

Foolhardy disregard laughs at wise exhortation
And arrogant contempt is blind to forewarning.

Judiciousness waves desperately at prudence,
Warning against false steps improvidently taken
And underlying menace blindly disregarded.

Ego-driven judgments, mindlessly foolhardy,
Crash, tyres spiked, shredded and made infirm.

Entitlement

The nets gifted to you gather fish in your sleep
While your brethren toil in the darkness.
The mountains that they climb
Are all rocky and steep.
Yours are streamlined, and with a harness.

You wait, eyes shut, for the fruit to drop.
They sweat while you break your gilded toys.
They are forced to climb to the tree's top,
But build while you savour your own voice.

Cosy in the comfort of your acquired opulence,
You primp in worldly over-indulgence.
You give conflicting signals
Of pretentious congruence,
Not assimilating their diligence.

Your voice may be deep, but it doesn't ring true.
The tones of a master.
They are made to take smaller steps behind you
And, yet, they walk faster.

You label yourself superior to others
Though they all exist as your sisters and brothers.

In the face of deprivation, they keep their dignity.
Your avarice will be a stigma for antiquity.

Why does your easy road not make you humble?
Prepare yourself to face your worst fears.
One day, your clay fortress will crack and crumble
When your entitlement disappears.

You will scream
For the handouts you are accustomed to
When your golden easy-chair turns into tin.
Your swagger will stagger, they will no longer hear you
And tantrums will replace your biased-win grin.

Hinder

———

Innocence stifled by hoary perceptions
Remains shuttered behind glass windows.
Pontificating caution barnacled over time
Engenders shackling circumspection.

The relentless wheel blindly trundles,
Trampling springtime bountifulness.
The tethered sapling pleases the eye
But its natural inclination is smothered.

Why deaden the shimmer of silk
As it searches for its rightful lustre?
What can the cane teach the seedling,
Other than atrophied contemplation?

The grip of gnarled fingers strangles,
Curbing the pulse of renewal.
By determining the flow of life,
We hinder the cause that links us.

Suffocating

———

Enfeebling barricades that choke ambition
Satisfy the obstructionist's paranoia
But send out echoes of emptiness.

Arms meant to reach out in wonderment
Hang limply by the side,
Impaired by life-sucking tentacles.

Manhole-covers, in umbrella-charades,
Dim the radiance of hopeful anticipation.
The venturesome soul is dispirited,
Its ebullience handcuffed to dominion.

Ambition flickers, then falters,
Its purpose rendered uncertain
In the face of suffocating control.

There is no sky for clipped wings
To wheel and circle unrestrained,
No emancipation beckons the impeded.

The barrenness of the treadmill prevails.

Relentless feud

———

The relentless feud between the said and the unsaid
Spurns the counsel of a mediating Godhead.
Thought in word battles word in thought,
An interminable, tumultuous war is fought.

Malevolence, with a throat-grasp on level-headedness,
Taunts reason stumbling blind-folded in darkness.
Prejudiced judgement scorns celestial light,
Shunning its shield in the self's calamitous fight.

Prudence is pinned to the wall of delusion
While cunning devilry entices exclusion.
Shunning the extended hand of wisdom,
Aspiration connives with flawed martyrdom.

Split seconds through narrow lenses,
Ample hours spanning unimpeded senses -
They face away from each other, at odds,
Paying heed only to their own hostile gods.

The unfamiliar

We squint behind our eyelids
As we stare at the unfamiliar.
REM in broad daylight.
None the wiser for what we learn
On our heads-down journey.
Snippets gathered from thin air
Exist in rarefied elevations,
Fulfilling status quo notions
Of fly-by-night glances
Perceiving a vindicating potpourri.
God's posture becomes invasive
In the presence of hate.

VI

WISDOM GAINED

All good

———

In the spotlight's shadow
A peripheral, insignificant, irrelevant face
Smudged into the throng.
… your moment's around the corner.

Rejection dripping off the ceiling.
With, not of.
Relegated.
… let it ride.

Inspiration like a rolled-up mat
Stagnating dully, unnoticed.
… no cause for concern.

Joe Average.
Semi-occasional abbreviation.
A minor acronym.
… come to terms.

Everyone sits on the spectrum.
OCD, undulating minds,
Restrict, repeat, detach, repeat…
… let's hold hands.

Dribbles, quibbles, foibles.
Inaudible syllables.
Nibbles, not bites.
… ups and downs.

Sometimes scrunched, increasingly hunched.
Turbid head, vacuous eyes, ageing.
… just lean back.

From soft whispers in youthful embrace
To thoughtful proximity over time.
In the end,
Just semi-anchored, uninspired passengers, grey.
… silver lining.

All flowers surrender their colours in time.
Birds fly, birds die.
... as they must.

Ever-deepening lines.
The paths and roads of life's journey.
Divots, ditches, trenches in mirrors.
... wisdom gained.

Spending years building wings
To help your children fly
And then they fly away.
... nothing wrong with that.

You're a greengrocer's apostrophe.
A misused semi-colon.
A full-stop.
... leave it and live.

Thoughts in turmoil, in disarray.
A tsunami of words, incoherent shambles.
... good with the bad.

Clever thoughts truncated mid-speech.
Pen capitulates and forsakes you.
Friends talking over you.
... duck's back.

Muffled fulfilment.
Whispered bird-song in a cage.
... chin up.

Frozen trigger-finger.
Adrenaline in torpor.
Inertia rules.
... mañana

I don't matter, I can't, I'm undeserving, degraded.
GIFs.
... Oprah Winfrey.

No match for a blowtorch.
Aspiring?
Only a brief, sputtering, sluggish flicker.
... you'll see the light.

Sidelined opinions, overlooked kindness.
Obliging eyes unnoticed.
... it's all good.

Shed the squeeze

———

Freedom is a boundless champaign.
Sing, think, love unconfined.
Shed the squeeze, discard the enclosures
And tap the abundance that abounds within.

Dislodge the thoughts that bar you,
The key is in your hands.

Be deft in ignoring dissuading voices,
They serve only to curtail ambition.

Why sit in silence?
Why padlock your thoughts?
Why conceal your feelings?
Let the prayerful cloister themselves.
You can soar and still be God's child.
Be good, do good, for that is all.
Preachers' tenets should not forestall you.

Your life is not meant to be confined.
Come out from under the coconut-shell,
The fronds will show you more than you see.
Nourish your inner voice to outdo the outer

.

Standing shoulder-to-shoulder, singing in time,
Only fetters your proclaiming strides.
Step out, step forward, step ahead.
Power over you is yours alone.

The skyline offers more fulfilment
Than that which possesses your feet.
Be reborn and flutter lightly in colours,
Unburdened by the density of deterrence.

Two staircases

———

That into which we are born

Comes with two staircases,

One to the loft, the other to the cellar.

At points, both doors unlatch,

Separately or simultaneously.

The choices that we make,

To venture high or low,

Determine our joys and our regrets,

Some transient, others abiding, all opportune.

Be aware of their fertility,

For they can guide you on your path.

Acceptable

———

To flicker dimly in peripheral light;
To accept the ordinary
And embrace the commonplace;
To be scarcely noticed and recognised
Without craving importance;
To be a minor voice in a massed throng
And a trivial accessory in a dance troupe;
To approach success with detachment
And not desire fame;
To live life, not grasp it,
And conform, not demand;
To read avoidance as blood-letting,
Not blood-shedding;
To stand by and watch the tide at flood
And not be drained by the misery of missing out;
To then drift unobtrusively into the shadows
And live a placid life of waning relevance;
To, finally, arrive at the culmination sedately,
Without lingering like a festering, cankerous sore –
Is to be content with the acceptable.

Not you

———

Do not presume
To nag your precious, recalcitrant ones,
However well-intended you are,
And yet be loved by them.
Invade their space with good intentions
But wear their angst with acceptance.

Sweet as your words may be,
Prepare yourself for their indifference.
The rebels in them
Should not impair your affection,
Nor their remoteness dampen your devotion.

Tell them truths that appeal to them,
Not the truth you see.
Do not abandon your sanguinity
When faced with their reproach.
Be all things benign
When assaulted by their wrath.

Though they keep their distance,
Hug them from afar.
If your consternation bursts their bubbles,
Let your back bear their whips.

It's about them, after all,
Not you.

No more parenting

There is a glow parents feel
When their children are open to communication
And a dispiritedness
When they remain closed books.
Sometimes, both sensations blend into each other
As they ebb and flow, embraced by undying love.

They seek the advice that suits them,
Not that which you want to give.
Keep your door open
Even if they shut theirs.
They make the best students.

It is what it is
And they are who they are.

You held them in your arms,
Then by their little hands.
Find it in your heart
To let them find their feet.

They're your world
But comes a time when you're less a part of theirs.
No more parenting, just parents.

Over time, entitlement abates
And a peaceful relevance
Embraces the inherent design.

New

Even if your flesh remains unchanged,
Wear your new clothing with pride.

Even if your memories hark back,
Regenerate yourself in the now.

Even if your mind is anchored,
Soar with the spirit of ebullience.

Even if familiar sounds resonate,
Open your untrained ear to the untried.

Even if your heart yearns for the known,
Let your soul tread new paths.

Goodwill

Good will come from goodwill.
Therefore, leave some behind,
Wherever your feet may venture.
It will not cost you a fortune,
Nor will your coffers be filled,
But the spirits of those touched
Will shower their blessings,
Knowingly or unknowingly,
On you, or on those you know,
Or on strangers, near or removed.
So, don't save your goodwill
For a rainy day but let it pour
Out of your willing hands
Into the lives of the unrewarded.

Pockets

Keep your hands in your pockets
If sinister omens portend calamity.
Keep your hands in your pockets
If awful misfortune lies awaiting.
Keep your hands in your pockets
If their soothing touch is scorned.
Keep your hands in your pockets
If your acquaintance is not sought.
Keep your hands in your pockets
If detachment is what you seek.
Keep your hands in your pockets
If poison is not your meat.
Keep your hands in your pockets
If your battered soul desires peace.
Keep your hands in your pockets
If temptation manifests its scheme.
Keep your hands in your pockets
If your spirits have lost their zest.
Keep your hands in your pockets
If seeking answers instigates tests.

Keep your hands in your pockets
If you wish to avoid incrimination.
Keep your hands in your pockets
If you wish to elude aggression.
Keep your hands in.
Keep your hands pocketed.
Keep your hands safe.
Keep your hands.

Her unsubdued mind

———

The years did not diminish her canvas.
She had lived her youth in straight lines,
But her bent fingers were her winding journeys,
Holding on to her eye-balling life's sinuous paths.

Through the sideshow
Of dealing with losses and gains,
The abundance of colours coursing through her veins
Were rainbow-companions, fearlessly palpitating,
Multi-hued defences against pernicious gaslighting,
Deleting enforced subscriptions to pseudo MOUs.

She surrounded herself with a dam against adversity,
Meeting tides of malignancy and pain with fortitude.
God's hues, both glorious and grim,
Journeyed with her,
Scripting her enlightenment on earth's surly miseries.

Her unsubdued mind danced with her wearied body

On the motionless wheels of her nest

And both sang dirges and songs of acknowledgement

As hazy eyes pondered the boundless unknown,

Deciphering a yet-to-be-completed crossword puzzle.

V

AN INNER DIN

Subdued

———

Creeping into empty spaces
Where feelings we hold dear coursed,
Diversion glides soundlessly,
A vanquishing trip-wire.

Disquiet ousts genteel sentiment,
The oblivious mind
Caught unawares.

Affection frets around a silent vacuum,
Pacing in bewilderment,
Furrow-browed.

Relentless weariness drains resolve
Like the sands in an hourglass.
Sombre shadows benumb the soul,
Draining its essence of its lustre.

The subdued spirit
Lies listless on its trampoline,
Its vitality curbed from within.

Gossip

The gossiping tongue,
The nexus of schadenfreude.
Lips, ears, squirming words,
Screeching whispers sowing spite,
Lusting ears craving more,
The rancid clan that gyrates stealthily,
Spewing ill-will.

Unreasoning malice, laced with venom,
Scheming to incite rancour.
Swirls of deception coil in concord around betrayal.
The pedlars of wreckage revel in their roguery.

Duplicity preys on trust,
Pitiless, remorseless, cowardly.
Overlapping faces slink in the shadows,
Smouldering malevolence behind the benign visage.
Confused Janus looks away momentarily.

The unsuspecting target struck,

The assailant slithers away

And quivers with impatient anticipation.

Words

———

Our words define us to ourselves.

Judgemental designators pontificating overbearingly
Stifle us.
Disdainful, self-righteous,
Disparaging halting disclosure
And mundane perceptions.
Deriding discontent in their elevated existence.
Exalted reproach immobilises aspiring inspiration.
Still-born expressions, deprived of breath,
Lie where they fall.

No soda fizz, no champagne bubbles.
Lightning and thunder
Strangulate fireflies and crickets.
Like fruits plucked before their time,
Quashed words are cruelly discarded by the scornful.

But their contempt exposes the decay in them

And the lantana

Could never be as blessed as the bloodroot.

Charity

Empty hearts that will not give,
In the vice-like grip of miserliness,
Exclude charity without a conscience.

Self-serving pleasures in tight fists.
Self-regarding ventures behind locked doors.
Self-seeking light shining inwards.

Backs turned, embracing only the self.
Meaningless smiles, concealing deception,
Mock goodwill.
A thin veneer of grace masks greed.
Geniality belies selfishness.

What is it that relegates outsiders to irrelevance?
Why is benignity restricted to the inner circle?
Divine light bypasses mean-spiritedness
And the shroud of small-mindedness reigns supreme.

Done

———

Head bowed, eyes downcast, gazing at emptiness.
Leaden thoughts, heart in turmoil, knotted.
Numbness deadens the mind, debilitates reason.

A vacuousness hangs limply on the realisation
That the done cannot be undone.
Careless steps taken burn trodden ground
And the fires flare unsparingly, unendingly,
Leaving a trail of calamitous embers
That cannot be extinguished.

Furrowed brow, heavy sighs, hollow eyes,
Shutting down any resolve.
The burden of guilt sits heavily on the shoulder,
Remorselessly weighing down the spirit.

Drifting deadwood, limp in dying flow,
Witnessing darkness closing in.
Obscurity-filled moments of daylight
Circle endlessly, closer and closer.

Taken

———

O, you child of this blessed land,
How cruelly you have been pushed aside!
The greedy hordes from distances afar
Have savaged your gentle presence.

Defenceless spotted gum and jarrah
Cannot stop the ravenous tide.
No defence against the grasping hand,
The spirit in you died.

Your beauty now bears a scar.
You have been stripped of your essence.
In your cupped hands, once a glowing star,
The flow of nourishment has dried.

Status

———

An entity with two parts,
One exalted, presumptuously vainglorious,
The other derided, disregarded underfoot.

Front row seats smirk at the gods,
Feasting on proximity that elevation cannot,
Gawking at goliaths' shadows tossing dwarfs
Where eucalypts lord over shrubs.

Raucous voices blare with thunderous force
Over muffled tones struggling to reach.

Dart boards in playrooms with keycards,
Signalling who can and who cannot,
Provide access to exclusive targets.

The potential of ambidexterity is discarded,
A limp rag snuffed out by power over-reach.

Ignorant

———

What you listen to in your head
Are just lies in demonic shade.
Fabrications, of envy bred,
By which the ignorant are swayed.

Each truth that you, with contempt, shred
Is corrupt blood through which you wade.
You allow yourself to be fed
With tales that make alignments fade.
Like poison, such malice will spread,
Slicing the guiltless with a blade.

Dead jade, thread frayed, bled aid, dread spade.

Busker

———

What keeps you going?
You are in the mix, out of it,
A stone in crossing streams.
Unturned faces, hurried paces,
Just ears cocked to the familiar.
Splashing tyres in pouring rain
Drench schoolgirls' skirts.
Straining against your ball and chain -
Talent in spurts.

Nothing is showing.

No bouquets, no brickbats, where you sit,
Just grey ponytail themes.
Empty bases, nowhere places,
Your future likely nonlinear.
The frenzied dance of scarred fingertips
Is gnarly gliding seen only by the easy hand.
Your voice is arid, your imitation smudged,

Your youth hollower than your takings -

Wasted tatters.

Off-key pauper.

Deviant

———

The weight loaded on slaves' shoulders
Shudderingly satisfies
And the racing mind's momentum
Scuttles unhindered.
The sense in the space of self-ownership creates itself,
Shunning justification for its existence and meaning.

Thoughts that flow uncurbed
Ignore the wind as it blows,
Buffeting branches and lashing leaves where they lie.
What light the sun brightens and the moon mellows
Goes unseen
Because beguiling shadows elbow their way through.

Melodious singing
Struggles against the impermeable deaf,
The singer's plaintive voice no more than white noise.
It is the standing up that tallies with the sitting down
But the marriage of movements crumble at the knees.

However compelling philosophies are

In their crystal balls,

They have no home

Where the past gapes deviously from frames.

Connection

Where voices reigned and laughter rang,
The chitter of fingers monotones in silence.

Mute reverberations behind barred windows
Shunt shuttered shortcuts in swirling displays.

Immobile faces and entrapped eyes fixate,
While preoccupied ears remain etherised.

Waxed leaves overlook labouring raindrops,
Their veins engrossed by the throb of diversion.

Unmoved hills pay no heed to wispy clouds
Whose wistful blessings go unnoticed.

Tense

———

What ticking bomb sits on the brink of exploding?

What is dammed inside that verges on bursting?

What shudders on the threshold of insanity?

What tautness disfigures sensibility?

What uproar pummels the mind?

What lies hidden behind?

Is it because of scars?

Is it in the stars?

Is it blood?

Word?

Less.

Tightness.

Plus and minus.

Patently superfluous.

Brewing storm looming.

The receptacle of sanity fuming.

The lit match flickers over the fuse.

The strained rubber band stretches in abuse.

Perpetrated paralysis constricts burning ambition.

Contradicting voices devastate with dire indecision.

No

———

The extent to which you confront 'No'
Determines the depth of your hope.

Reluctance thrives on uncertainty
Like barnacles that fiercely prevail.
Failure beckons on the road to success
If you veer from that which is extant.

Guilt, the churlish wayfarer, waits,
Sticking out its foot to hesitant strides,
Leaving the diffident floundering.
Indoctrination habituates the young
To observe with conditioned eyes.

Fault and praise swirl like starlings,
Murmuring their intent to finger those
Whose dogmas are held responsible.

Phobia

———

Trepidation's grip usurps composure,
Strangulating discerning logic.
Tendrils of tightness coil themselves
Suffocating, constricting, throttling.

Unfathomable panic drains composure,
Instantaneously gripping the heart
With the cold, awful hand of horror.
Agitation rises in a mad crescendo,
Thumping the manic drums of hysteria.

Reason, pummelled by an inner din,
Disintegrates into raw fragments.
Judgement freezes, counsel in disarray,
Stupefied in desperate dread,
As rationality staggers and implodes,
Disintegrating on unforgiving shards.

Sad closure

———

Hardened layers encrust surfaces
That thrived, silky-smooth, once.
Gentle thoughts that shone love
Are enmeshed in snarled disarray.
Tired smiles reflect sad closure,
Telling of unresolved intentions.
Nothing remains of soft affection,
Lying buried under inevitability.
Harmonious voices grow harsh,
Coarsened by abrasive discord.
Free-flowing expectations freeze
In the face of unanswered prayers.

Too late, the scramble for vigilance.

Assumed success falters, crashes,
Shattering hope into little pieces.
Homely rapport awaits its end
As it lies, immobile, on the pyre.
All that sparkled, day and night,

Is now in ruins, dusty, crumpled.
The music of youthful laughter
Tosses and turns in bumpy sleep,
Nodding head plaguing slumber,
As respite sneers from a distance.

Outdated

———

When that which is jaw-dropping
Becomes everyday and routine,
It impacts like outdated lingerie
Pushed ever farther into shelf-recesses.

The momentous hangs around awhile,
Displaying its attractions to gapers,
And then packs its bags and retires,
Leaving its footsteps in the mud,
Noticed, or otherwise, by their depth.

The jaw reels itself in, keyed up,
Waiting for its next bungee jump.

Obscenities

Obscenities are flung with loose abandon
Into the unguarded face of common decency,
Like sucker punches, jarring self-assuredness.
The victim reels unsteadily, a dumbstruck fawn;
The victimiser sprays incessant invective,
Assailing pacifism with relentless profanity.

Repulsive crudity jangles nerves with impunity,
As unbothered minds mouth odious utterances.
The obtuse bellow them like public defecations,
Rumbling, booming, erupting, discharging,
Accustomed to commonplace vulgar habitude,
Unconcerned by the coarseness they display.

They are blaring intrusions of corrupt clamour
That gratify in moments of ungoverned outburst.

But their profanities grow customary with time,
Repeated obscenities becoming mere noises,
Throw-away lines as conventional as blinking.

Yet, in the minds of the abashed disinclined,
These repugnant words swirl uncomfortably,
Prowling by the hatchway, agitating, harassing.
When the dams burst and commotion froths,
They are devoured by the sneering hordes
Who feast on the capitulation of the new arrival.

Ash

___

The pointy-rounded end of the ash, as she inhaled,
Nudged the shrouded shadows of her tortured past,
Reminding her of what lay behind her degradation,
Of the abuse she suffered in her defenceless days.
Blinded dolls mutely witnessed innocence stripped,
Broken cymbals' muffled begging went unheeded.

As the smoke spirited out through her trembling lips,
Her tortured soul counted the scars of desecration.

Darkness descended on her face.
She flicked it into tiny pieces.
They drifted in the air, clueless, puny spirits,
Baffled by their short, collective lives.

Then the breeze lifted
And took them their separate ways.

Lake

———

Your gross waters,
Camouflaged by the shimmering sun,
Falsify sparkling reflections of shoreline forests.

You placidly gloss over traumatised vegetation,
Disguising troubled Nature's maligned hues
In distorted liquid mirrors that deceive
With fake serenity.

Gentle breezes, lured by the fetching views,
Are burdened with painting over a blemished canvas,
Brushing dispirited blues and greens into a slow sway,
A sentimental dance
With whispered sighs for pristine days.

Powerless

————

The tree, in the shadow of which we sit,
Does not choose to be burned by the sun.
Paralysed against all that nature hurls at it,
It is stripped, sundered, ripped from earth.

Where are its limbs to ward off calamity
When the dissevering chainsaw appears?
How helpless against pitiless assailants,
Its semblance of strength just an illusion!
Like the dog, when it knows the end is near,
Does the tree's soul, too, surrender quietly?
Majesty, inevitably, is torn from its throne
By forces possessing the might it does not.

Its guardian spirit lies alongside, powerless,
Whispering its last rites, bidding it farewell.

Frenzy increases

The known and unknown in the cry lie hidden.
Questions agitate around it, seeking information,
But neither lock nor key has become available,
As is often the case with that which is desired.

The searching flow piles upon itself, congested,
Suffocating, halted at the unbreachable levee.
Its frenzy increases with its inability to abate
And it thrashes uncontrollably in its passion
To find a seething entry that is denied an exit.

Crescendo upon crescendo of helpless screams,
Yet the affliction of imprisonment remains cold.
The unsubdued clamour remains unexplained.

Ownership

This old earth does not claim ownership
The way we do.
What superior religion existed and clashed
Millions of years ago?
What straight-and-narrow preened itself
Before we appeared?
Language, song, apparel were not defined
As they are today.
No borders nor passports, no orders nor laws
Defined day or night.
What awful reckoning awaits the arrogant
When ownership is lost?

Two souls

———

Each nod between two souls hides its own truth.
Each formulates realities
Within its own world-wisdom.
Secretive machinations meant to keep the other out
Hide behind the sheer of fake, duty-bound consent,
Drawn out and held together
For the sake of appearance.

One is one's own audience as one treads the boards,
Made up and costumed in a smoke-and-mirrors turn,
With eyes and lips staging private performances
Behind a gossamer curtain.

Night disguises as day and days are pretend-nights,
Swaying to thunderclaps on a sultry afternoon.

Ghostly whispers rushing hurriedly past the ear
Ring doorbells in the dead of night
With leaden fingers,
Caressing taut faces that reflect dim memories of love.

Music, reduced to a monotone behind closed doors,

Plays shamelessly in a sham performance

When on display.

Doors

———

Doors. Portals. Enter. Exit.

The familiar and the unfamiliar cohabit.

Knowing the unknown.

Not knowing the known.

The pervious and the impenetrable,

Swinging into each other.

I hate a vacuum.

I often live in a vacuum.

Unhinged familiarity.

A protruding, duplicitous knob.

The fault lies in the wall.

I mean, there's no light-switch or movement-sensor

To brighten up the room.

Doors turn their back to me

And obstruct my decluttering.

The eye's ever-deepening obscurity.
Staring unblinking at brightness.

When I reach out for me,
Darkness becomes darker.

A distant dot

———

Threading the past into a forlorn rope,
She skips, friendless,
Ignored by the cold-shouldering PA.
To get, she gives, retribution for ease,
Shards on her footing.

Sleep does not pacify the soul
In a built-in cupboard,
An all-consuming crematorium
Where clothes shroud death
And ash imitates stardust.
Her role is that of a distant dot,
A mask without a face.
Counter-clockwise pronouncements
Thud a meaningless design,
Decibels in the darkness.

Discarded by broken patterns,
Living outside Nature's code,
She hears screeching sirens.

Configured music plays outside,
Blocking its ornaments from her.

Cupped hands hold emptiness.
She is denied her many gods
By disharmonious singing bowls.
Only the four compass bearings
Recite mantras for her salvation.

Yearning for appeasement

———

Whispering cacophonies,
Why abuse in mirrored doses?

Fleeting moments of calm,
Plucked unceremoniously
From trembling twigs,
Tumble in confusion.

Clashing cymbals
Drown out mellow tunes.

Encroachment is a tomb
From which faith gazes
Longingly
Through pinhole grilles,
Yearning for appeasement.

VI

DANCE IN UNISON

Soul mates

———

Such wonderful and eventful years
Since we got married yesterday!
Two ships, side by side,
Meandering through seas calm and rough,
Never losing sight of each other.

Looking back, it wasn't all that long ago
When, really, so much has gone by.
Through many lives and many places,
Hand in hand we've walked.
Through different moments,
Some simple, some grand,
We've cherished each other's presence.

And, so, we move along with time,
Letting it gently leave its mark on us.
The experiences we've had, the highs and the lows,
The joyful and vexed faces of drama,
I would not change them one bit,
For they have been with you.

We occupy the same space,
We take each other's place.
Even back and forth
We embrace growth,
Earthy and ethereal.

We are soul mates
And the soul has no use-by date.
You are my comfort – nice!
You are my clarity – super!

Solitude

———

Solitude often brings with it a quiet hush,
A calm healing of the pugnacious soul.
Gentle breath softly serenading
Dreamy melodies to soothe the restless spirit.

Undisturbed stillness appeases the preoccupied mind.
Unhurried thoughts meander languidly, noiselessly.
A peaceful sense of languor
Coaxes strained consciousness
Into the realm of daydreams.

Serene tranquility flowing delicately
Through leisurely reflection,
Like the wispy surface sands of dunes at dusk,
Drifting sleepily in whispering desert breezes.

Drooping eyelids usher the senses
To the edge of slumber.
Becalmed by the solace of mellowness,
The soothed mind slips, undisturbed, into quietude.

The caress of restfulness,
Lightly lulls the mortal being
Into welcome drowsiness,
Repose.

Friend

———

Dear friend,

Kindly excuse any trespass my words may engender.

Should I unwittingly offend with hurtful statements,

It is not my intention.

It is because I enjoy your company

That my feckless tongue blurts unthinkingly.

I would not, otherwise,

Because there is no joviality in indifference.

Being relaxed in your presence

Leads me to babble unkind utterances thoughtlessly

I may sound uncharitable

During moments of camaraderie

But blame it on unconscious carelessness.

It is in my stars.

Forgive me, the fault is mine,

Unintended as it is.

I am not mean, neither improper nor uncouth.

You are important to me.

Strength of spirit

The flowers in the flames that burst in the sinews
Cradle the strength of spirit
And illuminate the depths of emotion.
Sturdy limbs display intensity ablaze -
How powerful the body's instruments!

Summer and Winter dance in unison,
Reflecting the Sun's majesty.
A mighty tenacity springs forth,
Embodying a noble tumult
Which pounds earth, body and soul.

Impassioned eyes burn with potency,
And clarion voices spring from fervent tongues,
Deep and earnest reverberations of passion.
A powerful spiritual presence, singly and together,
With hypnotic power thunders.

A tender tranquility

———

Your gentle tinkling notes, as I contemplate the rain,
Strings of diamonds shimmering in the street-light,
Clink with a tender tranquility that calms.

Faint distant thunder soothingly harmonises,
Creating contentment in the softened dimness.
The spine feels a tingle when the rain and you mingle,
Tempting emotions out into the open.

You return the turbulent soul to timely sanity,
Temporary it may be, yet so uplifting.
Thinking transcends into heightened dimensions
In the night, alone in your ambient company.

The glinting raindrops,
Dancing in the nighttime breeze,
Accompany the entrancing tunes you plink.
Praise the nimble fingers tangoing on your tones,
May their bountiful talent multiply tenfold.

Pace

———

Touch all gently, with a soft calmness
That drifts on undemanding thought
And cradles a languorous grace.
Seek contentment at a serene pace
For there is no battle to be fought
And tranquility is a gift of stillness.

Be the dandelion seed, undisturbed
As it floats languidly, at peace.
With unhurried steps, at ease,
Turn your face to the gossamer breeze.
Find tranquility in the restful fleece.
Let quietness be at leisure heard.

Drifting log

———

Rather a drifting log than a grand yacht,
Free to be part of the natural flow.
No burly maintenance, no anchor knot,
Unhindered by manuals or bulky cargo.

A humble respite for the nature-dweller
That comes and goes, a tired traveller.

No boisterous clamour of man and machine,
Only the ocean's lapping and swishing.
No human passion, clashing to demean,
Just sky and sea, nature's happy plaything.

Lightly skipping waves of all persuasion,
Protected by the god of compassion.

Guided only by companion wind and tide,
Not enslaved by the engine or oar.
Taken on journeys to shores untried,
Not destined for the ocean floor.

Forest bathing

Knots and armour where smooth bark once flexed,
Lofty majesty soars, regal and resplendent.
Life-giving seeds that once were not,
Thrive, guided by Nature's decree,
Generating slender saplings,
Heralding majestic domes.

Mother earth embraces unhurried, snuggling roots,
Nurturing and nourishing them
As they burrow and trek away from the source.
An enduring kinship prevails.

The sky welcomes gently spreading, verdant green.
Sojourners and dwellers of feather and fur,
Greeted by extended arms, bring tales
Of faraway palaces
And find rest and solace in abundance.

Gentle breezes rustle through the leaves,
Lifting sacred fragrances into the air.

Shinrin-yoku beckons, forest bathing cleanses,

Healing body and mind.

Expanse outpaces time.

Gems

Nestled quietly in Nature's havens lie gems.
Tiny drops of sky and ocean,
Nursed by earth,
Mirroring the lustre of celestial orbs,
The shimmering silk of the fluid sea.

The passion and tumult in their dawn,
The intense fervour of the core heartbeat,
The ardour of fire, the patience of time –
Crowning in serene hues of brilliance,
Veins throbbing with scintillating radiance,
Vivid, vibrant, prismatic rainbows -
Transcendence unveiled,
Adored by the common eye.

Hold on to them

———

Hail their existence, for they complete yours.
Touch them gently with nurturing empathy.
Feel their pain in a world devoid of sympathy.
Soften your heart against remorseless apathy.
Cry for them when cruelty ends their course.

Hold on to them, and they will hold on to you.
The earth holds them, and they hold the earth.
They are your family, from birth to birth.
Their existence surely reflects your worth.
Rejoice in their world, for their voice is true.

Sands

Beach sands that softly yield underfoot
Hold steadfastly to timeless secrets.

Hidden tales that stretch across endlessly
On polished expanses soothed by the sea
Are rhythmic whisperings at each union,
Early and late kisses and caresses
Echoing an ancient togetherness.

Staying the course decreed by the universe,
Gliding layers ebb and flow in synchrony.

Each grain that pirouettes in calm and turbulence
Harmonizes with the mysteries denied us.

When

______

When a storm churns blindly in our midst,

Remember the calm.

When barbs threaten to rip us apart,

Hold on to the balm.

When fires flare with venom in us,

Use God-given charm.

When the menace of anger bodes ill,

Safeguard against harm.

When the tempest batters hatches,

Be the tranquil palm.

Your footprints

Your footprints fade there,
Even as they deepen here.
Your voice then, a faint echo;
Now heeded, a clarion call.
Your shadow lengthens and grows,
Strengthened by what it used to be.
What you have left behind
Will always cherish you.
What you have embraced
Now nourishes you.

What life delivers

———

From your land of five rivers,
You crossed the seven seas,
Taking what life delivers,
Never brought to your knees.

Your strong calloused hand
Harvests earth's sweetness.
You travel the gritty land,
Bringing far-flung souls gladness.

No companion but your horse.
No wayside home but your cart.
Misty eyes flicker over the source
Still evoking the beat of your heart.

Plunderers ignore your worth.
Inconsequential subordinate.
Vetoed brotherhood at birth.
High colour, pigmentation and hate.
How the will in you prevails!

One Truth in the face of abhorrence.
Your steel is described in tales
Of valour, bloodshed and sufferance.

And when they see your courage,
Their loathing turns into acclaim.
Your dignity, your carriage,
Your mettle - they honour your name.

An ancient wisdom moves around you,
Of spirits that once enveloped the land.
They softly speak of a life they knew,
Of Nature's blue seas, green trees and red sand.

So, be one with the soul of Dreamtime.
Respect the Earth that nurtured your brother.
Air is the Teacher (message sublime),
Water, the Father and Earth, the Mother.

AUTHOR BIO

Malaysian-born **Chamkaur Gill** is a retired academic in Australia, having taught at high schools and universities in Malaysia and Australia for more than forty years. Prior to his retirement, he taught at Bond University in Australia in the areas of English for Academic Purposes, Applied Linguistics and Literature. He has also had a number of academic papers, which deal with these subjects, published in a variety of journals. In addition, he has written a book dealing with the history of Sikhs on the Gold Coast. Chamkaur Gill's latest ventures are in play-writing and play-directing, including the staging of his play, 'Void', in mid-2021 on the Gold Coast, Australia.

His interest in poetry dates back to his school days but it was only after retirement that he took up independent creative writing seriously. This collection of poems, in which he explores a variety of human-interest issues, represents his first foray into published poetry.